P9-AQH-989

THE YEATS COUNTRY

SHEELAH KIRBY

THE YEATS COUNTRY

*A guide to the Sligo district and
other places in the West of Ireland
associated with the life and work
of W. B. Yeats*

with drawings by RUTH BRANDT

THE DOLMEN PRESS
SLIGO: J. M. KEOHANE

*Set in Times Roman type and printed and published
in the Republic of Ireland at the Dolmen Press Limited
North Richmond Industrial Estate
North Richmond Street, Dublin 1*

First published August 1962
Second edition, revised, July 1963
Reprinted, July 1966
New edition, revised and reset, 1969
Reprinted, 1977

*Published in the U.S.A. and in Canada by
Humanities Press Inc.
171 First Avenue, Atlantic Highlands, N.J. 07716*

ISBN 0 85105 333 5 THE DOLMEN PRESS
ISBN 0 391 00737 8 HUMANITIES PRESS INC.

*Grateful acknowledgement is made to Senator Michael
B. Yeats and to Miss Anne Yeats for permission to
quote from the work of W. B. Yeats in this book.*

Text © Hildegarde O'Connor 1977
Illustrations © The Dolmen Press Limited 1977

SHEELAH KIRBY

AN APPRECIATION

Those of us who were fortunate enough to visit Sligo in the early years of the Yeats International Summer School will remember Sheelah Kirby. She it was who, always from the background, was the moving spirit who set her seal upon those early years.

Sheelah Kirby was born in Sligo and, as the wife of a well-known doctor, lived her life there. She was always an active member of that part of the community concerned with Irish, and especially local, cultural interests and activities. She was proud of Sligo and its long history, its saints, poets, heroes and legends. Not only did she love all those places that W. B. and Jack Yeats had loved and known a generation earlier; her knowledge was detailed and exact. She writes with the authority of a life-long familiarity with all local antiquarian and archaeological matters; and it is upon the accuracy of local knowledge that all historians must finally rely. She was for many years an active member of the Sligo Field Club and for a time its President; she knew every site, every local tradition, from the remote past down to the present. To her these things were more than information, they were part of herself, and of her world.

On my first and subsequent visits to the Yeats Summer School I was among those fortunate enough to be taken by Sheelah Kirby to the places she knew and loved; for her generosity in sharing these things was as great as her own love for them. She was always ready to drop everything — and her life as a medical auxiliary was a busy one — and drive me in her mercurial little car, to climb

the hill of the Hawk's Well (it was she who discovered this well on a remote hillside as the
original of the miraculous site of Yeats's play) or
to explore the archaeological sites of Carrowmore
or the Bricklieve mountains; to enjoy the solitude
of Streedagh strand, or to show me those houses
of the Middletons and Pollexfens that W. B. and
Jack Yeats have made famous. But for her they
were part of the whole texture of Sligo and its
past and continuing life.

She knew and loved Yeats's poetry; but she
never allowed those of us who came from other
countries to forget that the Irish Renaissance rests
on immemorial foundations within the unbroken
continuity of Irish history. There were bards in
Sligo centuries before Yeats; poets and saints,
heroes and kings; from legendary people merging
into mythology, to families she herself remembered. These were no less part of the living culture
she inherited than were those names that brought
most of us to Sligo. From her rich knowledge of
these things, from her love of every hill and
stream and strand, church and ruin and holy well,
she has written this guide to the Yeats Country.
It is her record of the things she knew and loved,
of places consecrated not only by the poets and
saints of Ireland, but by the continuing life of the
culture she so generously shared and so accurately
transmitted. Sheelah Kirby died in 1975; and this
book, now reissued with her final revisions, is her
best memorial.

Kathleen Raine

CONTENTS

MAPS

In addition to the outline map on the following pages,
the following supplementary information may be useful.

The half-inch scale Ordance Survey of Ireland map,
sheet 7, covers in detail the area in chapters I - VII and
is recommended to readers using this guide in the Sligo
area.

The total area covered in the book will be found in
sheet 3 of the quarter-inch scale Ordnance Survey of
Ireland.

A folder on Sligo town and district is available at
the Sligo Tourist Information Office and provides a
useful street plan.

BASED ON THE ORDNANCE SURVEY BY PERMISSION OF THE MINISTER FOR FINANCE

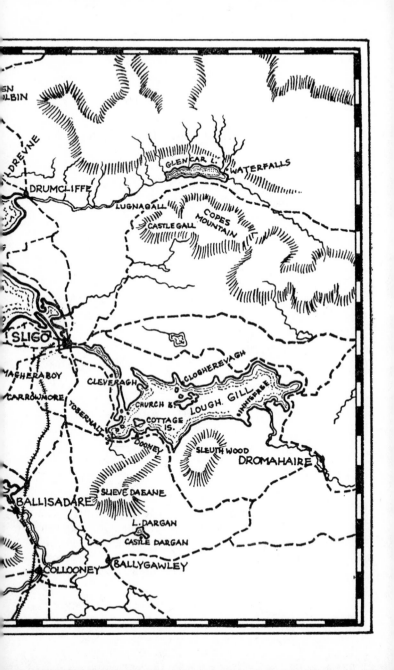

for
Rosalind and Hildegarde

One's verses should hold, as in a mirror, the colours of one's own climate and scenery.... (and) make every lake or mountain a man can see from his own door an excitement in his imagination.

w. b. yeats: *Ideas of Good and Evil*

I

THE SLIGO BACKGROUND

History and Tradition   Poets and Scholars
Saints and Scribes

The area surrounding Sligo, now linked by close association with the life and works of William Butler Yeats, is also connected with many centuries of Irish history and scholarship.

Such local place names as Moytirra, Keshcorann, Traig Eothaile and Ben Bulben occur and recur in the mythic tales of pre-Christian Ireland. Many of these tell of the constant wars between the men of Ulster and the men of Connacht, who time and again fought out their battles on the strands and mountains of Sligo.

This part of Connacht, now called The Yeats Country, had known centuries of poetry and learning, much of which had come near to extinction. Something, however, of the old tradition was tenaciously retained in popular story-telling and music, and then towards the end of the nineteenth century, scholars began to study and publish this wealth of half-forgotten Gaelic literature. The Irish Texts Society was founded by some of these scholars to collect and edit early manuscripts. All this was happening when Yeats was a young man, and he too became aware of the richness of that Gaelic literature which had inspired James Clarence Mangan and Sir Samuel Ferguson. Yeats and his friends established the Irish Literary Society in London in 1892. The object of this Society was the appreciation and critical study of Gaelic literature.

All this activity stimulated the work of local

historians, each actively collecting and recording the traditions of his own area. Sligo was well served by William Gregory Wood-Martin and Father Terence O'Rorke, both well known to William Butler Yeats. He had a detailed knowledge of their work and he wrote appreciatively of the part played by O'Rorke in introducing him to the forgotten Gaelic poets of Sligo.

In his later writings he was to recall how this introduction to Gaelic literature prompted him to think of creating an Irish *Prometheus Unbound*, with Saint Patrick or Saint Columcille, Oisin or Fionn, as the central figure. The interest he developed was quickened by the work of Standish O'Grady and Lady Gregory who were giving new life to the old Irish heroes narrated in 'the dry pages of O'Curry and his school'.

In many parts of Ireland at this time a similar renaissance was in progress. County Sligo, however, was doubly fortunate. In the first place, its stories and folklore were rescued from oblivion. This in itself was a valuable achievement. But over and above its regional importance, this re-opened vein of Gaelic legend inspired a great poet. William Butler Yeats took from the scholars of his native county the fables, myths and magic of a long hidden Ireland; in return he won for Sligo an honoured place in every textbook of literature, and gave to the world poetry of enduring genius.

Even in the earliest centuries Sligo was stirring. Cromlechs, stone circles, and cairns from those times exist in large numbers across the county. Storytellers breathed life into these monuments, peopling the district with ghosts of Maeve and Ailill who came with their armies from Cruachan

(Rathcroghan) in County Roscommon to invade Ulster, as well as with the heroic figures of Cuchulainn, Fionn, and Oisin, and those of the lovers Diarmuid and Grainne.

The earliest biographers of Saint Patrick mention some of the ancient place names of this part of North Connacht. The ruin of an old church in Drumlease at Dromahaire is said to be on the site of a Patrician foundation. Patrick had a disciple named Bron and Killaspugbrone 'the church of Bishop Bron', on the sea's edge under Knocknarea is named after him.

Patrician and earlier memories merge in the story of Oisin, a returned leader of the Fianna, that fabled pre-Christian band of warriors and huntsmen. Oisin on his return from Tir-na-n-og slipped from his fairy horse and found himself a wizened old man, puzzled by the unfamiliar Christian Ireland which surrounded him. In Yeats's narrative poem 'The Wanderings of Oisin' the meeting takes place at the foot of Knocknarea.

Sligo also figured in the Golden Age of Monastic Ireland. This was the period of the Ardagh Chalice, the Tara Brooch, the Cross of Cong, the Moylough Belt and that great triumph of Irish art—*The Book of Kells*.

Cul Dreimhne near Drumcliff now called Cooldrumman, was the location of the 'Battle of the Books' fought in 561 A.D. *The Cathach,* a fragmentary copy of the psalms, according to tradition the copy made by Colum Cille in his own hand, is said to be the cause of this early battle over copyright, leading to the saint's exile. The story still retains a strong imaginative appeal, especially the final judgement of the High King: 'To every cow its calf, to every book its copy.' *The Cathach* is now preserved in the Library of the Royal Irish Academy, Dublin. In the year 563 Colum Cille or Saint Columba, the name by which he is known to many, sailed to the island of Iona, off Scotland, where he established a great missionary movement, which has secured for that island an honoured place in the history of Western Europe.

In the Irish legend Saint Columba is not only a man of God, but also a poet and an exile, the common lot of so many of his compatriots down the centuries. He returned to Ireland, to attend the Convention of Druim Ceit in 575 where it is said he defended the poets against a threat of banishment. Friendship for poets is part of the Columban tradition. In Adamnain's life of Colum Cille, written at the end of the seventh century, it is recorded that when a poet visited the monastery of Iona, it was the custom to invite him to entertain the monks by chanting his poetry to them.

The early Annals came from the monastic schools and were the work of monks who wrote down the old myths and legends. With the Norman Invasion and the decline of the old Celtic monasteries, the making of the great manuscripts passed to lay scholars. Theirs had been an oral tradition of learning; they were the old order of the *fili*, heirs to the druids of pagan times, the custodians of poetry, history, and law. As time went on the word *file* came to mean poet. To be known as 'the son and a grandson of a poet' was to enjoy a title of distinction. These lay scholars worked under the patronage of a local king or chieftain.

In this fashion *The Annals of Lough Ce,* now in the library of Trinity College, Dublin, were copied, in the second half of the sixteenth century. They were abstracted from the *Book of the O'Duignans* for Brian MacDermot, the last Prince of Moylurg, by O'Duignan and other scribes, in his island castle. The O'Duignans were hereditary Chroniclers to the MacDermot and Erenaigh of Kilronan. The castle known as The Rock is an island in Lough Key (Loch Ce), near Boyle in north Roscommon, where Yeats dreamed of having his 'Castle of the Heroes'.

Hereditary learned families belonged to the aristocracy of early Irish society; they were not only poets: they were also judges, prophets, and historians.

The O'Huiginn (Higgins, O'Huigini) who held estates at Achonry and Kilmacteige in County Sligo, were among the most distinguished of these families. There were illustrious poets among them from the thirteenth to the eighteenth centuries. The fifteenth-century poets Maelcealchlain O'Huiginn and Tuathal O'Huiginn, were of this lineage, while the famous Tadhg Dall (blind) O'Huiginn has been described as 'the most celebrated poet of the late sixteenth century'.

The O'Cuirnins were hereditary poets and historiographers to O'Rourke of Breffni. They founded a school on Church Island, Lough Gill, where they worked at their manuscripts. The church from which the island took its name was destroyed by fire in 1416. The library containing the books and records of the O'Cuirnins was lost.

Another family of hereditary poets were the O'Dalaigh (O'Dalys). One of them, Muireadach Albanach (the Scot) O'Daly lived at Lissadell, later to be the home of the Gore-Booths. Muireadach, however, had to seek refuge in Scotland, after he slew O'Donnell's tax-collector who had angered him. He was restored to favour and his home, by writing poems in praise of O'Donnell, who was so pleased that he granted the poet land and patronage.

The O'Donnell name is also associated with poetry and learning. One poet of that name was the early sixteenth-century Prince of Tir Conaill, Manus O'Donnell, who lived at Ballyshannon, just across the Sligo border in County Donegal, and was the author of a life of his kinsman Saint Colum Cille.

Some of the great source-books of Irish history and genealogy were compiled in the county of Sligo. These and other famous compilations date from about the year 1400, and include enough valuable and diverse information to justify their description as 'mediaeval libraries'.

At Castle Firbis, Lecan near Enniscrone, a school of history grew up round the Mac Fhirbhisigh (Forbes) family, and from there came the great books that took their names from the place. *The Great Book of Lecan* was compiled about 1416-18, under the direction of Giolla-Iosa Mor Mac Fhirbhisigh, and is now preserved in the Royal Irish Academy; *The Yellow Book of Lecan* by Giolla-Iosa Mac Fhirbhisigh dated about 1391, is now preserved in Trinity College, Dublin. *The Book of the Genealogies of Ireland* (1585-1671), now in the library of University College, Dublin, was compiled by Duald Og Mac Fhirbhisigh, the last of these hereditary historians. He lived and worked in Dublin for many years and collaborated with the antiquarian, Sir James Ware. *The Book*

16

of Ballymote, now in the Royal Irish Academy, takes its name from the castle of Ballymote, the home of Tomaltach Og MacDonagh, Lord of Corann for whom it was compiled by Manus O'Duigenan, Solomon O'Droma, and Donald Mac Egan.

The Annals of the Four Masters (1630-1636), perhaps the best known of all the old books, were compiled by Michael O'Clery, a monk of the Order of Saint Francis and a refugee from Donegal Abbey after the English conquest of Tir Conaill. He was assisted by Peregrine O'Clery, Peregrine Duignan and Fearfeasa O'Mulconry. *The Annals* were compiled at Bundrowes, near Bundoran, and are dedicated to Fergal O'Gara, Lord of Moygara, who financed this great work which took five years to complete.

The Book of the O'Hara is a collection of thirty-eight bardic poems. The dunaire or poetry section of the manuscript is prefaced by genealogical and biographical tracts in prose. The chief scribe was Tuathal O'Huiginn but the more famous Tadhg Dall O'Huiginn also contributed to it. The book is unique among Irish manuscripts because the original vellum manuscript remained in the possession of the descendants of the chieftain, at whose request the work was undertaken. He was Cormac O'Hara Buidhe, Lord of Leyney, and his descendants, the O'Haras of Annaghmore, County Sligo, are the present custodians of this late sixteenth-century work. In 1951 the Dublin Institute for Advanced Studies published the original text from a photostat copy in the National Library of Ireland.

As the Gaelic social order died, much of the

17

knowledge contained in these great manuscript volumes faded from memory. After the siege of Limerick in 1691, Patrick Sarsfield, with the flower of the Irish aristocracy, crossed over to the Continent, where they were not debarred, as Catholics, from positions that matched their birth and rank. Those that remained lived as outlaws, many of them sheltering in woodlands that were soon cut down. The passing of this Gaelic world was lamented by its poets.

Yet something of the past was remembered and passed on by wandering bards and musicians, among them Thomas and William Connellan of Cloonamahon, County Sligo, whose early seventeenth-century airs have been praised by the collector Hardiman. Some of their compositions won popularity in Scotland and were given new titles there. These include *Molly McAlpin* and *Molly St. George.*

A familiar wanderer on the roads of north Connacht in the eighteenth century was the blind harper Turlough O'Carolan, who was welcomed by poor and rich, by native Irish and English planter. He composed tunes in honour of the families who befriended him, the MacDermots, the O'Conors, the O'Harts, the Corkrans and the O'Haras and also for the Croftons, the Coopers, the Irwins and the Wynnes. He died at Alderford, the home of The MacDermot Roe, just outside Ballyfarnan. This was the house of his friend and patron where he had always been received as one of the family. The burial of O'Carolan has become a legend in the district; the wake lasted four days, and an enormous concourse, including ten harpers, attended the funeral ceremonies. He is buried in the tomb of The MacDermot Roe in the ruined church of Kilronan, and the inscription on a stone over the graveyard entrance reads: 'Within this churchyard lies interred Carolan, the last of the Irish bards. He died March 25th, 1738. R.I.P.' It was placed there by Lady Louisa Tenison, of Kilronan Castle, about the year 1858.

II

SLIGO TOWN

The town of Sligo is rich in Yeatsian associations. Many of its streets and buildings are mentioned either in Yeats's own works or in writings about him. A typical example is the graceful Italian Renaissance Town Hall, which dates from 1864. The poet wrote a great deal about his uncle, George Pollexfen, and recalls how on one occasion Pollexfen, though a Unionist, paced up and down the Assembly Room in the Town Hall with Parnell when that great leader of the Irish Parliamentary Party in Westminster came to Sligo to contest an election. Yeats wrote much about his uncle, always with affection and admiration:

> . . . I think of old George Pollexfen,
> In muscular youth well known to Mayo men
> For horsemanship at meets or at racecourses.

When George Pollexfen died, it was an end to years of melancholia and hypochondria, a sad finish to the life of a man who had been in his youth a superlative horseman and a substantial personality.

> . . . Masons drove from miles away
> To scatter the Acacia spray
> Upon a melancholy man
> Who had ended where his breath began.

Pollexfen, who under his nephew's tutelage had become a member of the Order of the Golden Dawn, ended his days as a melancholy astrologer. He lived at one time in Quay Street, 'close to a disreputable neighbourhood', until he became so disturbed by noise and quarrelling under his windows that he moved. This noisy neighbourhood was almost certainly The Burrough, one of the

many overcrowded and insanitary alleys in which the poor of Sligo lived. The thatched cottages of the old Burrough have disappeared and all that now remains is the cobblestoned Fish Quay which was built in 1822; the entire length is not more than 200 feet. It replaced the primitive quay of the Port which was under the walls of the Cromwellian Castle and just below the mills. The Town Hall now stands on the site of the Castle, and the Silver Swan Hotel and stores at its rear now occupy the side of the old Pollexfen saw-mills. The 1904 Post Office building has replaced the fish market. In *Stories of Red Hanrahan*, Yeats describes the blind men and the fiddlers who found lodgings in the Burrough.

The firm of W. T. & G. T. Pollexfen had offices on both sides of the west end of Wine Street. A glass and slated turret stands on the roof of the stone building at the Wine Street-Adelaide Street corner. From there the poet's grandfather, William Pollexfen, trained a telescope on his ships coming up and down the river. The first home of the Pollexfen grand-parents was a modest house in Union Place, beside the family stores, but they had moved from there to the fine residence outside the town named Merville, long before their

daughter married John Butler Yeats. Union Place
leads downhill into Pern Mill Road. Yeats wrote
in *Reveries over Childhood and Youth*:

> All my dreams were of ships; and one day a
> sea-captain who had come to dine with my
> grandfather put a hand on each side of my
> head and lifted me up to show me Africa,
> and another day a sea-captain pointed to the
> smoke from the pern-mill on the quays rising
> up beyond the trees of the lawn, as though
> it came from the mountain, and asked me if
> Ben Bulben was a burning mountain.

Members of the Yeats family were always happy
to come back to Sligo from abroad. Frequently
they came by boat and arrived at the Sligo Quays.
The poet wrote in 'Under Saturn':

> You heard that labouring man who had served
>   my people. He said
> Upon the open road, near to the Sligo quay—
> No, no, not said but cried it out—"You have
>   come again,
> And surely after twenty years it was time to
>   come."
> I am thinking of a child's vow sworn in vain
> Never to leave that valley his fathers called
>   their home.

At the quays the Yeats children disembarked for
their holidays in Sligo from one or other of their
grandfather's steamships, the 'Sligo' or the 'Liver-
pool', after a thirty-hour voyage from Merseyside.
At that time the family lived in London, and the
boy Willie Yeats and his sister came close to tears
when they talked of Sligo. They 'longed for a
sod of earth from some field they knew, something
of Sligo to hold in their hands'. He remembered

22

the Sligo Quays again in *On the Boiler,* published
in October, 1938, a few months before his death:

> When I was a child and wandering about the
> Sligo Quays I saw a printed, or was it a
> painted notice? On such and such a day the
> great McCoy will speak on the old boiler.
> I knew the old boiler, very big, very high, the
> top far out of reach, and all red rust. I wanted
> to go and hear him for the boiler's sake, but
> nobody encouraged me.

From the Quays one looks across the river to
Charlemont House, on its grassy green hill. This
house was built by Charles Anderson, and for
a time William Pollexfen resided there. Some of
Yeats's letters carry this address. The house was
later known as Ardmore, became a girls' school,
and is now a nurses' home. One can imagine the
old man watching his ships at Sligo Quays from
this commanding site. The sailors, pilots, and boat-
men who swarmed about the port in those days
may be seen in the early sketches and drawings
of Jack B. Yeats which reflect that period, when
sail was giving way to steam.

It was in Saint John's Church on 10 September,
1863, that William Pollexfen's eldest daughter
Susan was married to John Butler Yeats, the poet's
father. Saint John's, renamed The Cathedral of
Saint Mary the Virgin and Saint John the Baptist,
was built *circa* 1730 to the design of the German
architect, Cassels, but nineteenth-century altera-
tions have since obscured the original design.
Hazelwood House is a better example of this architect's work. Saint John's stands on the site of the
Hospital granted in 1235 to Clarus Mac Mallin,
Archdeacon of Elphin and the Canons of Trinity

Island, Lough Ce. There is a tradition that the present Church replaced an earlier one built in the seventeenth century. Sir Roger Jones, the first English Governor of Sligo Castle, is buried there. He declared in his will 'my body I commit to the earth, in my tomb, in the Chappel I lately erected in the parish of Saint John's in Sligo'.

Yeats's grandfather, William Pollexfen, in his old age walked every day from his home at Rathedmond to supervise the building of his tomb in Saint John's Churchyard. In his elegy 'In Memory of Alfred Pollexfen' the poet remembered many of the Pollexfens. It is a short walk from John Street to the Market Cross, by the butcher's shop of *The Celtic Twilight* story which is now a chemist's. The Memorial at the Market Cross is to the men who fought and died in the 1798 Rebellion. This was the event that inspired the play *Cathleen ni Houlihan*, which fired many of the young men who fought in 1916. Years later Yeats was to write

Did that play of mine send out
Certain men the English shot?

Sligo Abbey, or more correctly the Dominican Friary, is the only building which survives from the town's medieval past. It was founded in 1252 by Maurice Fitzgerald, grandfather of the 1st Earl of Kildare. He also built a Castle at Sligo, which is believed to have stood at the east end of the present Castle Street. The Abbey was accidentally destroyed by fire in 1414 and subsequently rebuilt. Its present ruinous condition dates from the sack of Sligo in 1641. The ruins consist of a nave and choir with central tower. On the south side of the choir are eight deeply-splayed windows of thir-

teenth-century workmanship. Beneath the beautiful fifteenth-century east window is the high altar, also fifteenth-century; it is the only sculptured example to survive in any Irish monastic church. The O'Conor Sligo monument of 1624, on the south wall, is considered to be of fully developed Renaissance style. Its kneeling figures depict Sir Donogh O'Conor Sligo and his wife Lady Elinor Butler, daughter of Edmond, 1st Baron Dunboyne, and widow of Gerald, 14th Earl of Desmond who was killed in 1583. The nave retains three arches on the south side and the north wall, in which is the elaborate altar-tomb (1616) of the O'Creans. The tower supported by lofty arches and groined roof should be noted. The stone rood-screen, immediately west of the tower, is an interesting and uncommon feature of the church. The cloisters, on the north side of the nave are almost perfect on three sides, in each of which are eighteen arches of beautiful workmanship, and elaborately ornamented pillars. On the north side of the cloister, on the upper floor, can be seen the corbel which supported a small oriel window, lighting the reader's desk in the refectory. The south transept, chapter house and domestic buildings are greatly dilapidated.

25

In 1641 both town and Friary were sacked by Sir Frederick Hamilton and Puritan troopers. It is believed that the friars were all killed, but, before the century was out their successors were back in the town. The Dominicans' long association with Sligo has continued up to the present day. During the eighteenth century they were often in hiding, and it was not until the early years of the nineteenth century that it was possible for them to build a small church, discreetly hidden behind the Pound Street houses. The ruin of this little building is still to be seen. Towards the end of the last century, the Order built the present Holy Cross Church in High Street.

As might be expected, the events of 1641 became the subject of the legend-makers, and Yeats made it the theme of his story 'The Curse of the Fires and of the Shadows':

> All the monks were kneeling except the abbot, who stood upon the altar steps with a great brass crucifix in his hand. "Shoot them", cried Sir Frederick Hamilton, but nobody stirred . . .

The story goes on to tell of the slaying of the friars and the sack of the church: and as the soldiers retreated:

> Before them were burning houses. Behind them shone the Abbey windows filled with saints and martyrs, awakened, as from a sacred trance, into an angry and animated life. The eyes of the troopers were dazzled, and for a while could see nothing but the flaming faces of saints and martyrs.

We are told too that the silver bell of the ruined Abbey lies on the bottom of Lough Gill, where it was deposited by Prior MacDonagh, to await better times. Only the perfect are privileged to hear the peal of its silvery notes on occasions when it rings over the town.

Corkran's Mall still retains a little of its eighteenth-century charm. The Linen Hall, built in 1764, is now part of the Imperial Hotel. Set in the wall of the hotel is a stone date slab 1782, the year Henry Grattan proclaimed Irish Parliamentary Independence. The fine eighteenth-century script cut on this stone may also be seen on many tombstones in the Abbey. The Corkrans who built Thomas Street and Corkran's Mall were ancestors of General Michael Corcoran of the Fighting 69th New York Irish Regiment.

As a young man Yeats published a story which he called *John Sherman*. The hero of this tale visits Sligo and stays at the Imperial Hotel, which is described in some detail. The Imperial looks out on the newly laid promenade which has been dedicated to the memory of John Fitzgerald Kennedy, President of the United States of America, to honour whose memory an inscribed stone has been set into the wall of the old bridge.

When Yeats went to Stockholm in 1924 to receive his Nobel Prize, he admired the city's seventeenth-century palace, noting that 'the windows, the details of the ornaments, are in the style that has spread everywhere'. He said that the palace reminded him of the Ulster Bank in Sligo, which he admitted he had hardly seen since his boyhood years.

III

SOUTH WEST OF SLIGO

Carrowmore   Knocknarea   Family Houses

A road south-west from the town leads to Merville, the house where Yeats lived as a little boy
with his grandparents. It is to this house his
thoughts returned in *Reveries over Childhood and
Youth*. It is now The Nazareth House, and many
small boys have found a home and kindness there,
but today it is mainly the old who seek refuge
within the large buildings which have grown up
around Merville. The road goes on to Magheraboy, no longer a country crossroads with a few
thatched cottages. Now suburban houses move
closer and closer to Carrowmore cemetery, a place
of particular interest to archaeologists, as it forms
one of the largest concentrations of megalithic
tombs in Europe. There were at least sixty-five
tombs in the area, now reduced to about thirty
sites. The tombs are of simpler construction and
lack the elaborate corbelled structures found at
Carrowkeel and elsewhere.

This passage grave cemetery is overlooked by
the mountain of Knocknarea (1,078 feet) crowned
by the great unopened cairn of Miscaun Maeve
which probably covers a passage grave. The cairn
is 200 feet in diameter and approximately 80 feet
high. This is the place of which Oisin spoke to
Saint Patrick, in 'The Wanderings of Oisin':

> Caoilte, and Conan, and Finn were there,
> When we followed a deer with our baying
> hounds,
> With Bran, Sceolan, and Lomair,
> And passing the Firbolgs' burial-mounds,

28

Came to the cairn-heaped grassy hill
Where passionate Maeve is stony-still . . .

Knocknarea, like that other limestone mountain,
Ben Bulben, is very much part of the mythology
of Yeats. The great unopened cairn on its summit
has always stirred the imagination. In a foot-
note to 'The Hosting of the Sidhe', Yeats writes

> Knocknarea is in Sligo, and the country
> people say that Maeve, still a great queen of
> the western Sidhe, is buried in the cairn of
> stones upon it.

Maeve, the Queen Mab of English folklore, was a
Celtic goddess who as Queen Maeve of Connacht
personified the mystic sovereignty of that kingdom.
The Maeve of Tara and Sligo would seem to have
been the Celtic goddess. At Rathcroghan in County
Roscommon, the seat of the Kings of Connacht,
Maeve becomes the warrior queen who with
Ailill reigned over Connacht and is one of the
heroic figures of the Irish Sagas. Near Maeve's
Cairn there are the remains of several tombs and
there are others on the slopes of the mountain.
There are many Knocknarea legends, and for the
reader of Yeats this is the 'Land of Heart's Desire',
the country of 'Red Hanrahan's Song about Ireland' and of 'The Hosting of the Sidhe'. It is told

that the warrior, Eogan Bel, received his death wound at the battle of Sligo in 537, and is buried on Knocknarea. His dying command was that he should be buried standing upright with his blood-red javelin in his hand and his face to the north, 'on the side of the hill by which the northerns pass when flying before the army of Connacht'. There is also the legend of the Spirit of the Mountain, who, it is said, appears only once in seven years, and takes the form of a sad female figure, weeping and showing signs of great distress.

The glen or Alt on the south side of Knocknarea is a deep cleft in the hillside, about one mile long and only about thirty feet broad, bounded on each side by steep cliffs and overgrown with trees and shrubs. It was called by the old people the Alt, which is the Irish word for a wooded glen, or cliff. Bulfin described it in 'Rambles in Eirinn':

> Soon after coming to the slope of the hill you meet one of the queerest, wildest, and most beautiful glens. It is a wondrously romantic freak of nature planted there in a cleft rock and walled off from the world, as if the Great Mother meant to lock it up and hide it away for her own use. It is thickly wooded, narrow and deep. The trees meet over the path in places and the ferns touch you as you pass. The spirits of Knocknarea must love it. One can fancy how they made it their own centuries ago. A mystic poet might dream his life away in it, holding communication with the hero dead of Connacht.

Yeats wrote:

> In a cleft that's christened Alt
> Under broken stone I halt
> At the bottom of a pit
> That broad noon has never lit,
> And shout a secret to the stone.

Nearby is Glen Lodge where Yeats and his Uncle George dined with old Cochrane of the Glen. He wrote about this dinner-table conversation in 'The Tragic Generation'.

Great waves crash on the shore at Strandhill, not far from Culleenamore. In ancient times, before the building of roads and bridges, the strand passes were used by the armies of Connacht and Ulster. As late as the year 1536 O'Donnell's army, marching from Tirconaill to the Battle of the Curlew Mountains, used the strand passes, camping at Lisheen near Culleenamore.

> The Red Branch camp in a great company
> Between wood's rim and the horses of the sea.
> . . . Cuchulainn stirred,
> Stared on the horses of the sea, and heard
> The cars of battle and his own name cried;
> And fought with the invulnerable tide.

Like Cuchulainn we can stare on the horses of the sea, from the shore at Strandhill. They are a splendid sight when a strong wind blows from the Atlantic with an incoming tide. Killaspugbron (The Church of Bishop Bron) is the most ancient in Carbury; it was founded by Saint Patrick, who placed it in the charge of one of his disciples, Bishop Bron, a native of Coolera. Saint Patrick, we are told, shed a tooth, which fell on the threshold of the Church. The tooth was enshrined and kept there. In the seventeenth century the Fiacal

Padraig (Saint Patrick's tooth) was the most vene-
rated relic in Connacht. The reliquary is now in
the National Museum, Dublin. Until recently this
was the traditional burial ground of the people of
Coolera. The family of Bruen, until recently so
numerous in the Rosses Point area, claim to be of
the same lineage as Bishop Bron.

Coney Island can be reached either by boat from
Rosses Point or at low tide by the Strand near
Scarden. Pillars mark the crossing to the island,
which is rich in legend and folklore. The island
is said to have given its name to the island in New
York Harbour. A Rosses Point man was captain
of the 'Old Arethusa' which sailed between Sligo
and North America, early in the nineteenth century, and it was he who christened Coney Island,
N.Y. after the little island offshore from his native
village. The old Coney Island families are the
Harans, Cartys, MacGowans and the Carters.

The strand continues on to Cummen and to the
rocks of Far Finisklin.

> The old brown thorn-trees break in two high
> over Cummen Strand,
> Under a bitter black wind that blows from the
> left hand.

There is little left of Cummen House, sometime
home of the Ormsbys and described in the *Travel-
lers' Guide to Ireland* (1839) as a very noble edi-
fice, with beautiful and extensive parks, gardens
and demesnes.

Thomas Ormsby of Cummen was buried in
Saint John's Church in 1662. The last Ormsby to
live in Cummen was Charles, Deputy Lieutenant
for the county from 1838 to 1849.

Even when Yeats and his Uncle George Pollexfen walked along this road from Thornhill, Cummen House must have been dilapidated. He described just such a house in *John Sherman*.

> About a mile to the west of the town he came on a large wood bordering the road and surrounding a deserted house. Some local rich man once lived there, now it was given over to a caretaker who lived in two rooms in the back part. Men were at work cutting down trees in two or three parts of the wood. Many places were quite bare. A mass of ruins—a covered well and the wreckage of castle wall—that had been roofed with green for centuries, lifted themselves up, bare as anatomies.

Willowbrook or Annagh on the north shore of Lough Gill was the seat of Philip Ormsby and his descendants; one of them, William Richard, 2nd Lord Harlech was Member of Parliament for Sligo from 1841-1852. The present Lord Harlech, British Ambassador to Washington at the time of the Kennedy Administration, is of this family and a descendant of the Willowbrook Ormsbys.

The Ormsbys also had a house at Cairns, overlooking Lough Gill from the south side. It was known as Belvoir, and has been in ruins for more than a hundred years. Yet another branch of the Ormsbys lived at Castle Dargan, and one of Yeats's relatives, the Middletons, married into this family.

Rathedmond was William Pollexfen's last home, and it was from it, in his old age, he walked every day to supervise the building of his tomb in Saint John's Churchyard.

Thornhill, where George Pollexfen lived, is just

across the road from Rathedmond. Yeats, writing of his Uncle's house, said it was 'an old three-storied house, with a small garden in front and a yard and field at the back, about a quarter of a mile into the country'. At that time these houses were on the outskirts of the town.

IV

WEST OF SLIGO

The Rosses

The road to Rosses Point winds by Charlemont House, and over Cartron Hill beyond which is a long, low, sea wall of which Yeats wrote in *Reveries over Childhood and Youth*—a tongue of land covered with coarse grass that runs into the sea, or the mud according to the state of the tide. It is the place where dead horses were buried. Sitting there my father read me the 'Lays of Ancient Rome'. It is still called Horse Island.

Towards Rosses Point the road follows the channel that runs from Sligo to the sea. Here the boy Yeats was shown one evening the lights of the outward-bound steamer with his grandfather on board. Next morning he heard the vessel was wrecked and eight men in it drowned.

Rosses Point is itself full of memories. It is best to go there when there are no crowds, in winter or early spring, at dawn or when the moon is full. The essence of this place is hidden in Yeats's verse, as in the lines

Or when along the wintry strands
The cormorants shiver on their rocks.

When the bell buoy is being lashed about in a storm, every Rosses Point man will know the 'gong tormented sea', which becomes 'a mackerel-crowded sea', when the silver shoals appear in the bay.

One cannot write of Rosses Point and not think of Jack Butler Yeats and his drawings in 'Life in the West of Ireland'. One of his drawings, 'Memory Harbour', is the frontispiece in the first edition of *Reveries over Childhood and Youth*.

The poet wrote of it:

> Memory Harbour is the village of Rosses
> Point but with the distances shortened and
> the houses run together as in an old-fashioned
> panoramic map. The man on the pedestal in
> the middle of the river is The Metal Man,
> and he points to where the water is deep
> enough for ships. The coffin, cross-bones and
> skull, and boat at the point of the head-land
> are to remind one of the sailor who was
> buried there by a ship's crew in a hurry not to
> miss the tide. As they were not sure if he was
> really dead they buried with him a loaf, as
> the story runs. My brother painted the picture
> many years ago.

The Jack Yeats sketches bring to life the old
days at Rosses Point. The Watch House, now in
decay, stands near the golf club-house. This small
house with its tall white flagstaff once played an
important part in the life of the village. From
here the pilots watched day and night for signals
from Raghley Head, and here Jack Yeats sketched
The Pilot. There are pictures of the pilot boat
rowed with vigour under the Metal Man; Henry
Middleton, The Squireen striding along a dusty
road; The Long Car, on which the front seat was
always reserved for George Pollexfen; the old
lady in the village shop; and the excited crowds at
the Back Strand Races, which were later transferred from the Lower Rosses to Bowmore.

Towards the end of his life Jack Yeats wrote
'I never did a painting without putting a thought
of Sligo into it'.

Yeats's great-uncle William Middleton owned
two houses, Elsinore Lodge at Rosses Point and

Avena House at Ballysadare, near the family flour mills on the far side of Knocknarea. Elsinore was built by a successful smuggler named John Black, who set several cannon outside it, as though to command the estuary. After his downfall the house passed to the Coopers, who sold it with all the land of Rosses Point, to William Middleton, in the year 1867. His son, Henry Middleton, a contemporary of Yeats, was an eccentric and lived alone at Elsinore where he kept a herd of Jersey cows, and peacocks on the green before the house.

> My name is Henry Middleton
> I have a small demesne,
> A small forgotten house that's set
> On a storm-bitten green.

When Yeats was a boy the Middleton family spent the winter at Avena and the summer at Elsinore, and it was with these cousins that he rowed in the river mouth and fished for skate and herring. He remembered one night, sailing home in the coastguard boat, just as the equinoctial gales were coming.

> Indeed, so many stories did I hear from sailors along the wharf, or round the fo'castle fire of the little steamer that ran between Sligo and Rosses, or from boys out fishing

that the world seemed full of monsters and marvels.

In later years the poet walked over the sand-hills with George Pollexfen. There were no golf links then, nor was there a road down to the sea. The Greenlands stretched far and wide like some undiscovered country, and the sea dashed against the rocks at Deadman's Point.

Pooldoy is a deep pool and a good anchorage, within the Bar in Sligo bay, where vessels some-times lie in wait for the high tide to enter the harbour. Yeats called the Formorian Giant in his story Dhoya and said 'he strode into a pool to his shoulders — the place where he stood is called Pooldhoya to this day' . . . Pool Dhoya is at the river mouth at Sligo.

The Pilot House in the last field near Dead-men's Point is just as Yeats described it in 'The Old Men of the Twilight':

At the place, close to the Deadman's Point, at the Rosses, where the disused pilot house looks out to sea through two round windows like eyes, a mud cottage stood in the last century. It also was a watchhouse, for a cer-tain old Michael Bruen, who had been a smuggler, and was still the father and grand-father of smugglers, lived there, and when, after night-fall, a tall French schooner crept over the bay from Raughley, it was his busi-ness to hang a horn lantern in the southern window, that news might travel to Dorren's Island, and thence by another horn lantern, to the village of the Rosses.

On the old maps Coney Island is called Dorren's Island.

38

Moyle Lodge, near the gates of Elsinore, was George Pollexfen's summer home, while Bowmore Lodge, next door, was another Middleton house. The Middletons believed that Elsinore was haunted by smugglers, and would often listen for the three taps upon the window-pane. All these houses look across the channel to Oyster Island, to Knocknarea and to the burial mound on its summit recalling the legend of Eoghan Bel.

There in the tomb stand the dead upright,
But winds come up from the shore:
They shake when the winds roar,
Old bones upon the mountain shake.

These lines are from 'The Black Tower', the mysterious poem Yeats wrote five days before his death in the South of France. In old age, it is said that the memories of childhood and youth become more vivid and recent events fade. More than any other part of Sligo, Rosses Point was the childhood paradise of the Yeats children, for it was there the long summer holidays were spent, at a time when it was the domain of their Middleton and Pollexfen relatives. 'The Black Tower', which is a source of much speculation, is full of images that seem to come out of Sligo Bay.

The lighthouse on Oyster Island and the other on the Black Rock reef must have been the first towers with winding stairs to stir his imagination. The Black Rock was built in 1835, on the site of an earlier beacon tower. The existence of oath-bound gangs of smugglers discovered at a public enquiry in Sligo, 1820, underlined the necessity for improvements in the lighting of the Bay. In those days, too, stories of the oath-bound Fenians were a cause of alarm for some and for others a beacon of hope. Then one day the Fenian banners appeared in Sligo Bay, in the same year as William Middleton became the owner of all the land between the Sligo and Drumcliff estuaries. Unaware that the Rising in the South of Ireland had failed, 'The Jackmel', a vessel of 200 tons, set sail from New York, with a cargo of 5,000 stand of arms and three cannon, in charge of a number of Fenian officers; on Easter Sunday 1867, in mid-ocean they fired a salute, and changed the name of the vessel to 'Erin's Hope'. It was manned by Irish-American soldiers, disbanded after the American Civil War. They arrived in Sligo on 20 May, 1867, and:

> One evening a hooker came alongside from which a man, who appeared to be a gentleman, got on board the brigantine. This person went down into the cabin, conversed with the officers, and told them a landing could not be effected at Sligo, after which he returned to the hooker and sailed for the shore. The ship left the Sligo coast on about the 26th May.

They were betrayed by an informer on board, and three of the officers were afterwards convicted and sentenced to long periods of penal servitude.

The Brassbounder by David W. Bone, a classic of the sea, contains a vivid account of what it was like to sail into Sligo port in a wind-jammer, towards the end of the last century.

The poet brought his friend A.E. (George Russell) to visit the area, which was reputedly a haunt of fairy. Together the two poets walked along the Greenlands, climbing the slopes of Barrnios-Aird, where they were encircled by the glory of five counties, and from where they would see

The light of evening, Lissadell,

Great windows open to the south.

Those who wish to visit the 'seven little lakes'
and the country of the 'Old Men of the Twilight',
should go along the Upper Rosses to the Catholic
church and then turn left, heading for 'out yon-
der', which is the only way the place is ever
described. This is an enchanting place of tiny lakes
and tufted reeds.

There is a lake down at Bowmore where star-
lings gather in the reeds; it inspired Seumas
O'Sullivan's poem, 'The Starling Lake'.

The Coney Island men who fished off the strand
at night, used to tell stories of the mermaids seen
there. The bell buoy in the bay can be heard at
times from the strand. When the wind drops, and
stillness spreads with a dove-grey mist over the
sea, then the sound of the bell comes over the
water

Saddle and ride, I heard a man say,

Out of Ben Bulben and Knocknarea,

*What says the Clock in the Great Clock
Tower?*

All those tragic characters ride

But turn from Rosses' crawling tide,

A slow low note and an iron bell.

There are caves at the southern end of the
strand. Rinn Point is at the northern end; this is
the *Far Point* of the Jack Yeats picture which now
hangs in the Sligo Town Hall. It is also 'the little
promontory of sand and rock and grass, the
mournful haunted place' of the stories in 'The
Celtic Twilight'. Here until recently there were
also caves and the wreck of an old schooner, now

41

buried in the sands. It is possible that in a few years the caves will be visible again for the sand banks shift with the winter storms.

From almost anywhere in this area, it is possible to see the face carved by nature on the southern end of Ben Bulben, but it is perhaps most visible from the Bowmore Strand where the fresh water stream runs into the sea. 'I have walked on Sinbad's yellow shore, and never shall another's hit my fancy.'

The Lower Rosses can be reached either by walking across the Greenlands to the lake at the northern end of Bowmore, or by taking one of the boreens that lead north from the road to Sligo Town. At Cregg you will see on top of a hill, a little square two-storied house, under one gable a dark thicket of small trees. This is Seaview, now Carroll's farm, where the poet's great-aunt 'Micky' lived. She was Mary Yeats, whose father had been Rector of Drumcliff, where he died in 1847. The widow and children of John Yeats had a house nearby, and some miles away, 'in a house by a ruined mill, with a stream flowing in front of it', lived another of Parson Yeats's sons, Matthew, a land agent, who had a large family of boys and girls. Yeats has recalled his boyhood visits to this long, low house at Rathbroughan, riding out to it on his red pony, to join his cousins in sailing toy boats on the little river near this still very attractive house.

V

SOUTH EAST OF SLIGO

Lough Gill, Innisfree, Drumahaire

Another Sligo area closely linked with the poet Yeats is that around Lough Gill to the south-east of Sligo town. The lake is surrounded by wooded mountains, and is rich in legends. If the weather is suitable, it should be seen by boat; this is easy to arrange locally. It is also possible to make the complete circuit of the lake by road.

From Corkran's Mall the road follows the river bank to Cleveragh, which was at one time the home of Colonel W. G. Wood-Martin, author of *A History of Sligo, County and Town* (Hodges Figgis, 1882) and other books regarded as authoritative works on the customs and traditions of the ancient Irish.

Cleveragh (the place of the basket-makers) is a reminder of an old craft, for the salley or willow rods were used for making baskets. The Salley Gardens are a well-remembered feature of the Sligo riverside, in the early years of this century. The people of the town have always held that these were the Salley Gardens of the Yeats poem. Yeats says that he based the poem on a few lines he heard sung at Ballysadare. There is no doubt that the folk singers of Sligo, Leitrim, and Donegal sang an older version of 'Down by the Salley Gardens'. Salley rods are still to be seen in the wooded park along the riverside, which continues on to the road that leads to Cairns Hill. The hill which rises to about 390 feet is capped by two cairns: according to legend they mark the graves of Omra and Romra, two chiefs who ruled over the city now lying under the waters of the lake.

The road passed close to the remains of the old Ormsby Castle, and across the river stately Hazelwood House rises above the trees. It was built in the eighteenth century to the design of Richard Cassells, and was the seat of the Wynne family. This wooded demesne, which stretched along the north-west shore of the lake, was at one time famous for the variety and profusion of its trees and shrubs. The rare arbutus flourished there and its splendid scarlet berries can still be seen on the shores of the lake.

> I went out to the hazel wood,
> Because a fire was in my head,
> And cut and peeled a hazel wand,
> And hooked a berry to a thread.

The Green Road goes from north to south across Cairns Hill and from its summit, the whole panorama of Lough Gill, its islands and surrounding mountains can be seen in all their splendour. The nearby cairn, screened from the road by a thicket of gorse, provides an excellent vantage point to look out over the town to the sea beyond.

Tobernalt (the cliff well), near the lakeside under Cairns Hill is often called the Holy Well and has been a place of pilgrimage from early times. The old, stone altar below the well is a penal mass rock, for it was here, in the penal times that the people of the countryside came to worship. They assembled here in the darkness of night to await the coming of the outlawed priest. The annual pilgrimage to Tobernalt takes place on Garland Sunday, the last Sunday of July. Crowds attend Mass at the well on that day.

From Tobernalt the road goes round the lake to Dooney Rock celebrated in 'The Fiddler of

Dooney'. From this rock also the visitor may look out over the island-studded lake.

Slish Wood is nearby on the next peninsula of the lake. Yeats wrote of it in *Reveries over Childhood and Youth*:

> My father read to me some passage out of "Walden", and I planned some day to live in a cottage on a little island called Innisfree, and Innisfree was opposite to Slish Wood where I meant to sleep. I thought that having conquered bodily desire and the inclination of my mind towards women and love, I should live as Thoreau lived seeking wisdom . . . I set out from Sligo about six in the evening, walking slowly, for it was an evening of great beauty, but though I was well into Slish Wood by bedtime, I could not sleep . . .

It has yet to be explained why he changed the name of Slish when he wrote of 'Sleuth Wood by the lake' in 'The Stolen Child' and again in 'The Heart of the Spring', a story which was praised by George Moore for the beauty of its prose. In the first edition of this story it is 'the wood of the sleuth hound' and in later editions 'sleuth wood'. The Forestry Department, the present owners of 'Yeats's Bed' in Slish Wood, have changed the name to Lough Gill Forest.

Innisfree (Inis Fraoich—the heather island), is the tiny island immortalised by Yeats in what is almost certainly his best-known poem, 'The Lake Isle of Innisfree'. When asked by some children 'Is Innisfree a real island?', the poet replied:

> Yes, there is an island called Innisfree, and it is in Lough Gill, Co. Sligo. I lived in Sligo when I was young and longed, while I was still as young as you, to build myself a cottage on this island and live there always. Later on I lived in London and felt very homesick and made the poem, "The Lake Isle of Innisfree".

The legend of the island tells of a young warrior named Free, from whom it takes its name. He was persuaded by the daughter of the chief to bring her some luscious fruit which grew on the island but was reserved for the use of the deities, and guarded by a dragon. He killed the monster but tasted the fruit and died. His sweetheart, in despair for the loss of her lover, also ate the forbidden fruit and fell dead across his lifeless body. They were buried together on the island. Innisfree is referred to in the *Annals of the Four Masters,* under the year A.D. 1244, when it appears to have been the site for the lake dwelling of a local chief.

He stood among a crowd at Dromahair;
His heart hung all upon a silken dress.

Dromahaire on the lovely river Bonet is surrounded by a countryside famous for its beauty and history.

It was the chief seat of the O'Rourkes (Princes of Breiffny) and the scant remains of their castle can be seen on the left bank of the Bonet. This is believed to be the site of the famous banqueting hall, for the chiefs of Breiffny were noted for their princely hospitality.

This was the subject of a celebrated song in Irish which Carolan set to music. Swift made a humorous translation of 'O'Rourke's Feast' which begins

O'Rourke's noble fare
    Will ne'er be forgot
By those who were there
    Or those who were not.
His revels to keep,
    We up and we dine
On seven score sheep,
    Fat bullocks, and swine.

The song celebrated the tradition of the Christmas festivities held in the Great Hall of his castle in Dromahaire by the famous sixteenth-century chieftain Brian O'Rourke, Prince of Breiffny, who gave shelter and arms to many of the Spaniards stranded on the Sligo coast after the wreck of the Armada (1588) and for which he paid with his life at Tyburn in 1591. Sidney described him as the proudest man he had ever dealt with.

The ruins of a castle built in 1626 by Sir Edward Villiers, brother of the Duke of Buckingham, form a boundary wall to the present-day residence called the Lodge.

On the left bank of the Bonet are the ruins of Creevelea Abbey, a Franciscan friary founded in 1508 — by Margaret O'Brien, wife of Eoin O'Rourke. The friars were banished in the seventeenth century but they returned in about 1642.

Dromahaire has been linked by legend with an event which changed the course of Irish history. It is a story which moved Thomas Moore to write 'The Valley lay smiling before me', and William Butler Yeats to write *The Dreaming of the Bones*. Dervorgilla, wife of Tiernan O'Rourke, eloped or was abducted by Diarmuid Mac Murrough, King of Leinster. Shunned by his neighbouring chieftains, Diarmuid applied for help to Henry II, who allowed the barons of Wales to sail for Ireland in 1169. Thus Thomas Moore sang of the heartbreak of Tiernan O'Rourke, Prince of Breiffny, as he was returning home from the north and looked out over the 'smiling valley'.

Yeats's ancestors were associated with Dromahaire. When William Pollexfen sailed into Sligo in 1883 on the 'Dasher', he came there to offer his services to a cousin of his, Mrs. Middleton of Dromahaire, whose daughter he subsequently married. Mrs. Middleton was a widow, and found

William's ability useful in her milling and ship-owning business. He later became a partner in the firm.

From Dromahaire the road follows the north shore of Lough Gill into Sligo Town, passing at some distance the elevated plateau known as O'Rourke's Table, which looks down over the 'smiling valley' of Thomas Moore's song.

A ruined castle stands on the lake shore, close to the road. It is the seventeenth-century plantation castle of the Parke family. It was used as an outpost by Sir Frederick Hamilton when he marched on Sligo in 1682. It is said that afterwards he arrested Captain Parke whom he suspected of disloyalty and of being 'a traitor in correspondence with the Irish'. A fragment of the old, sixteenth-century fortress of the O'Rourkes can be seen close by.

Clogherevagh, which means the place of the grey rock or stone, adjoins the old Hazelwood estate which continues along the lake shore into Sligo Town. Clogherevagh, the dower house of the Wynnes of Hazelwood, built of cut stone, blended perfectly into its surroundings of rare beauty. It is now the property of the Ursuline Order and shares the site with a large new building, which caters for the needs of St. Angela's Domestic Science Training College, established in 1950.

The largest island on the lake is close to the shore here. It is Inis Mor, or Church Island. This was the site of the sixth-century foundation of Saint Lomain. The island contains the ruins of a medieval church which replaced the earlier monastery. The church was destroyed in 1416. by a fire which also burned the priceless manuscripts of the O'Cuirnins, the hereditary poets of the O'Rourkes. There is an inscribed stone built into the wall on the inner side of the entrance door of the Church, which is said to be an ogham inscription. There is also a ruined medieval chapel on Cottage or Gallagher's Island near Dooney Rock. This was a Premonstratensian foundation of the first half of the thirteenth century, attached to Trinity Island, Lough Key. Across the lake from Clogherevagh, the bare slopes of the mountain rise above Slish, or Sleuth Wood,

> Where dips the rocky highland
> Of Sleuth Wood in the lake
> There lies a leafy island
> Where flapping herons wake
> The drowsy water-rats . . .

VI
SOUTH OF SLIGO
Ballysadare   Collooney   The Ox Mountains

Ballysadare takes its name from the rapids on the Unshin river that flows into the sea below the little town. It was originally called 'Easdara', 'the cataract of the oak'; or according to ancient legend, the cataract of Red Dara, a Formorian druid who was slain by Lewy of the Long Hand. It afterwards took the name of Baile-easa-Dara, the town of Dara's cataract. Yeats used this legend in the story *Dhoya*, one of his earliest publications. 'One evening Formorian galleys had entered the Bay of the Red Cataract, now the Bay of Ballagh.' In this work Yeats used the name Ballagh for Sligo.

The Middleton and Pollexfen flour mills are at Ballysadare near a salmon weir, rapids, and a waterfall. The Middletons lived at Avena House and Yeats stayed with them as playmate for his cousin George Middleton, but he wrote in *Reveries over Childhood and Youth*, 'it was more often at Rosses Point I saw my cousin'. It was in Ballysadare he heard from Paddy Flynn many of the 'Celtic Twilight', stories. Yeats described this old man as 'the most notable and typical storyteller of my acquaintance'. It was in this village also that he heard an old woman sing the original folk tune, which inspired his version of 'Down by the Salley Gardens'.

Collooney was the home of Archdeacon Terence O'Rorke, author of *The History of Sligo Town and County*, published by private subscription in 1889. Among the subscribers were Yeats's relatives:

51

Mr. George T. Pollexfen, J.P., Quay Street
Mr. W. C. Middleton, Elsinore.

Yeats learned a great deal of Sligo lore from these books. He acknowledged this when he wrote:

Father O'Rorke is the priest of the parish of Ballysadare and Kilvarnet, and it is from his learned and faithfully and sympathetically written history of these parishes that I have taken the story of Fr. John, who had been priest of these parishes, dying in the year 1793. He was a friend of the celebrated poet and musician Carolan.

Father John's story became 'The Ballad of Father O'Hart'. Another name in the list of subscribers to Father O'Rorke's History was that of Very Reverend T. S. Conmee, S.J., Rector of Clongowes Wood College. Father Conmee, who figured in James Joyce's *Ulysses* and *A Portrait of the Artist as a Young Man*, was a native of County Sligo.

The children's eyes
In momentary wonder stare upon
A sixty-year-old smiling public man.

It is the poet in this unexpected role that Lennox Robinson captured, briefly in his life of Bryan Cooper. We read of Yeats speaking from a platform in County Dublin, in support of Bryan Cooper, standing as an Independent candidate in the first Dail Eireann Election after the Civil War. He was the owner of Markrea Castle, near Collooney, and the head of the family, well known in County Sligo for more than three hundred years.

Tubberscanavin is a townland on the Dublin road near Collooney. 'He mused beside the well of Scanavin'. This is a countryside of wells or tubbers, all with their legends and folklore.

Tubberbride, near Collooney, may well be the Tubber of *The Pot of Broth*, for the famed horse fair of Carricknagat was at one time held at this well. It was the custom for people to come to pray there on the festival of Saint Brigid, the first day of February. Many came on horseback, the women and girls riding pillion, behind their men-folk. While the women prayed, the young men amused themselves running and jumping the horses. On these occasions horses were sometimes bought and sold, until finally it developed into more of a place of business than a place of prayer, the owners of the land objected and the fair was moved to Carricknagat.

At the present time, an air of mystery surrounds Tubberbride or the Well of Saint Brigid. There is a large rath or fort, under which is a souterraine, with entrance and exit blocked up; it is said that there are two chambers in the souterraine and in one of them there is a well.

The splendid sycamore tree which stands near the entrance to the larger chamber is, alas, beginning to show the ravages of time. In this remarkable tree there is a cavity which is always full of water, summer and winter, and is said to have healing properties. This has been called the well in the tree and has been mistaken for the true Tubberbride which is underground.

Tubberbride is on Mr. J. P. McGarry's farm on the Dublin road south of Collooney.

The Hawk's Rock (Carraig na Seabhaic) in the Ox Mountains near Coolaney is close to the strange well of Tullaghan. O'Rourke, writing in 1888, described the rock as an eyrie on the face

of the precipice, from which the hawks would come
whirling and screaming on the approach of an
intruder. Nearby is the steep Hill of Tullaghan,
famous for its well, which is one of the Mirabilia
Hiberniae, or Wonders of Ireland, in Nennius,
Giraldus Cambrensis, and O'Flaherty's 'Ogygia'.

> In Sligo district, on Mount Gam's high side,
> A fountain lies, not wash'd by ocean's tide;
> Each circling day it different waters brings,
> The fresh—the salt—from it alternate springs.

The book of Dinnsenchas gives the legend of Gam,
the servant of Eremon, who was slain on the
mountain, thus giving his name to Slieve-Gam.
His head was cast into the well, which thereupon
became enchanted, containing salt water at one
time and fresh at another, and ebbing and flowing
with the tide. The people of the district came here
to celebrate the great festival of Lughnasa. Saint
Patrick, hearing of this superstition as he was
leaving Tireragh, came to Tullaghan and blessed
the well, which then became a place of pilgrimage
for the followers of the saint.

Those who have tested the well, in order to
discover the truth of the legend, agree that the
water sometimes rises and subsides in a remarkable manner. The water is brackish, and unattrac-
tive to both the eye and the palate, and at times
seems to be almost dried up and grown over by
weeds.

There are three stone cashels on the hill, from
the summit of which one can look down on the
plain of Corann and out over Sligo Bay.

> I call to the eye of the mind
> A well long choked up and dry
> And boughs long stripped by the wind,

And I call to the mind's eye
Pallor of an ivory face,
Its lofty dissolute air,
A man climbing up to a place
The salt sea wind has swept bare.

This hillside breathes the very atmosphere of Yeats's play, *At the Hawk's Well*. Lough Achree, meaning Heart Lake, is in the Ox Mountains not far from Ballysadare, off the road to Beltra. A little further south in the mountain range, one comes on the smaller Lough Minnaun, close by Hart's house and farm.

O'Driscoll drove with a song
The wild duck and drake
From the tall and the tufted reeds
Of the drear Hart Lake.

The Strand of Beltra is often mentioned in Irish mythology as Traigh Eothaile. Sir William Wilde called it Tra Cuchullin (Cuchulainn's Strand) and quoted Beranger who toured Ireland in 1779 and stopped to draw a view of Cuchullin's tomb, a circle of stones twenty-seven feet in diameter, but much covered by the sand which the tides carry on it. It is said that this cairn existed down to 1858, and was one of the 'Mirabilia Hiberniae'. However, the Four Masters judged it to be the tomb of King Eochy, who was killed in battle there, while retreating from Moytirra. His pursuers, the three sons of Niamh, were also killed, and it was believed that the cromlech on the shore at Beltra was their burial place. This legendary strand, bounded on one side by the wild Ox Mountains and stretching across to Knocknarea, runs out into the Atlantic, where the setting sun turns sea and sky into a blaze of colour.

The dews drop slowly and dreams gather;
    unknown spears
Suddenly hurtle before my dream-awakened
    eyes
And then the clash of fallen horsemen and
    the cries
Of unknown perishing armies beat about my
    ears.
We who still labour by the cromlech on the
    shore,
The grey cairn on the hill, when day sinks
    drowned in dew,
Being weary of the world's empires, bow to
    you
Master of the still stars and of the flaming
    door.

A characteristic of Sligo Bay is the splendour of its sunsets.

In one of many notes on 'The Valley of the Black Pig', Yeats wrote: 'I have made the Boar without bristles come out of the West, because the place of sunset was in Ireland as in other countries, a place of symbolic darkness and death.'

Slieve Da Ein or The Mountain of the Two Birds: the folk tale of the Cailleac Beare or Clooth-na-Bare is given by Yeats in his notes to 'The Hosting of the Sidhe': he says that this legendary figure found for herself the deepest water in the world in little Lough Ia on top of 'the bird mountain in Sligo'.

Castle Dargan lies to the south of Slieve Da Ein, and was the home of the last of the Sligo Ormsbys. The poet wrote of this house:

56

Sometimes I would ride to Castle Dargan where lived a brawling squireen, married to one of my Middleton cousins. It was, I daresay, the last household where I could have found the reckless Ireland of a hundred years ago in final degradation. But I liked the place for the romances of its two ruined castles facing one another across a little lake.

Castle Dargan and Castle Fury: The squireen lived in a small house his family had moved to from their castle, sometime in the eighteenth century, and two old Miss Furys, who let lodgings in Sligo, were the last remnants of the breed of the other ruin!

There were those who told of seeing the ruin lit up and hearing sounds of revelry at night, and this is the way it is in *The King of the Great Clock Tower*.

O, but I saw a solemn sight;
Said the rambling, shambling travelling-man;
Castle Dargan's ruin all lit,
Lovely ladies dancing in it.

VII

NORTH EAST OF SLIGO

Glencar   Ben Bulben   Drumcliff

The road to Glencar goes up to the Mall to Calry Church and the Grammar School. It passes some tall, old houses with iron railings and stone steps, and gardens going to the riverside. Of these Yeats reminisced:

> Sometimes my grandmother would bring me to see some Sligo gentlewoman whose garden ran down to the river, ending there in a low wall, full of wallflowers, and I would sit upon my chair, very bored, while my elders ate seed cake and drank their sherry.

The Grammar School was opened in 1907, when the Incorporated Society took over the old Diocesan School, built large additions to it, and transferred their Primrose Grange School to Sligo. The original building dates from 1750. The Head Master of the School at that time was W. C. Eades,

> Many a son and daughter lies
> Far from the customary skies,
> The Mall and Eades' grammar School,
> In London or in Liverpool.

The Glencar Valley runs from east to west, between parallel mountain ranges of Slieve Carbury to the north and Castlegal or Slieve-ganbaistead (the Mountain without baptism) to the south. Approaching from Sligo Town one sees first the green mountain slopes on which graze many sheep; this is Lugnagall, the 'steep place of the strangers'.

> He slept under the hill of Lugnagall
> And might have known at last unhaunted sleep

Under that cold and vapour-turbaned steep
Now that the earth had taken man and all.

The road continues on under the precipices of
Copes Mountain, scene of the Protestant Leap, and
across on the mountain the spray blows high from
Sruth-in-aghaidh-an-aird—the stream against the
height. The waterfall is so called because the water
is sometimes blown upwards. It is seen to most
advantage after heavy rain with a stiff breeze from
the south.

'The cataract smokes upon the mountain side';
Yeats has described it perfectly.

From the high road one may look down into the
lovely valley, out into Sligo Bay, and across to the
mountain of *The Secret Rose*.

> One winter evening an old knight in rusted
> chain armour rode slowly along the woody
> southern slope of Ben Bulben watching the
> sun go down in crimson clouds over the sea.

This road which leads to Manorhamilton is
haunted by the ghosts of the local legend of the
Cromwellian Wars which Yeats wove into his
Secret Rose tale, 'The Curse of the Fires and of
the Shadows'.

> They had taken the road between Ben Bulben
> and the great mountain spur that is called
> Cashel-na-Gael . . . Suddenly they saw the
> thin gleam of a river, at an immense distance
> below, and knew that they were upon the
> brink of the abyss that is now called Lug-
> nagall, or in English the Steep Place of the
> Strangers. The six horses sprang forward, and
> five screams went up into the air, and a
> moment later five men and horses fell with a

dull crash upon the green slopes at the foot of the rocks.

Manorhamilton was called after Sir Frederick Hamilton, who figures in the story. His ruined baronial mansion, built in 1638, is the chief object of interest in Manorhamilton.

The better-known waterfall at Glencar is down in the valley near Siberry's cottage where Yeats and Arthur Symons stayed for a few days. This is the beautiful waterfall of 'The Stolen Child' and 'Towards Break of Day'.

A few hundred yards to the north, an untarred road winds its way to the top of the mountain. Half-way up this road a stile and path lead north into an echoing glen.

The Crannog on which there was a lake-dwelling can still be seen in Glencar Lake. In his fairy tale, *Dhoya*, Yeats writes of how Diarmuid built the crannog and 'hid his Grania, islanded thereon'.

This man-made island is said to have been the scene of a tragic event recorded by the Four Masters in the year 1029, when Hugh O'Rourke, Lord of Dartry and the Lord of Carbury and Angus O'Hennessy, Aireneach of Drumcliff and three score men of the nobles of Carbury were burned to death there. There is no sign of a dwelling-place now; only the diminished little island remains.

Leaving Glencar the road winds round to the Ben Bulben side. It takes its name Ben-Bulban, Gulban's Peak, from Gulban, son of Niall of the Nine Hostages, who was fostered near it. He was ancestor to the O'Donnells of Tirconnell.

Yeats more than once referred to the small white door in the limestone side of Ben Bulben, 'in the

middle of the night it swings open and those wild unchristian riders rush forth upon the fields'. This is the legendary country of Fionn and the Fianna and of the hunting on Ben Bulben ending in Diarmuid's fatal duel with the boar. It is consequently the setting of the final episode in the best known of epic love tales, 'The Pursuit of Diarmuid and Grainne'. On this mountain-side, one of the great tragedies of the civil war occurred in September 1922. Less than a month after Michael Collins had been killed in ambush in his native County Cork, six members of the anti-treaty forces lost their lives while engaged in combat with troops of the National Army; five young men of County Sligo and a son of Professor Eoin McNeill of Dublin. Eoin McNeill was co-founder with Douglas Hyde of the Gaelic League in 1893. Three months later William Butler Yeats was nominated to the first Irish Senate.

Narrow mountain roads lead down to Cooldrumman (Cuildrevne) scene of 'The Battle of the Books', and to Lissadell and the sea.

> When long ago I saw her ride,
> Under Ben Bulben to the meet,
> The beauty of her countryside
> With all youth's lonely wildness stirred.

Along these roads, Constance Gore-Booth, said to be the finest horsewoman in Ireland, 'rode to the meet or drove the horse tandem at full speed over Tully Hill . . .'

All around Lissadell and Raughley are Eva Gore-Booth's 'Little Roads of Cloonagh'.

The house at Lissadell is still lived in by Gore-Booths. Built in 1832, it is a plain Georgian house. Yeats first met the daughters of this enlightened ascendancy family in 1894. In 1927, thirty-three years later, he wrote, at Seville in Spain, his elegy 'In Memory of Eva Gore-Booth and Constance Markiewicz'.

This house was a symbol to Yeats of the ordered and gracious living which he found fitted in with his ideas about personal fulfilment and achievement. A couplet sums up his thinking:

How but in custom and in ceremony

Are innocence and beauty born?

Eva later helped to organise women workers in English textile factories: but continued to write poetry. Constance turned to politics, married Count de Markiewicz, became a leader of the 1916

Rising, and second in command of the unit which held the College of Surgeons, St. Stephen's Green, Dublin.

Streedagh Strand (a few miles north of Lissadell) saw the wrecking of three ships of the Spanish Armada. Don Francisco de Cuellar, captain of one of the ships, came ashore here and was succoured by the Mac Clancy at Lough Melvin and by Brian O'Rourke, Prince of Breiffny. He subsequently returned to Spain via Scotland and later published an account of his adventures in north Connacht, which has since been translated into English.

Innishmurray, four miles off the coast, has been uninhabited since October 1947, when the entire population, then reduced to fifty, came to live on the mainland. Up to that time the island had its own hereditary chieftain or king. The island is remarkable for its antiquities, some dating to pre-Christian times. It has been described as 'a museum of antiquities relating chiefly to the earliest period of the ancient Irish Church'. It is also renowned for its Clocha Breaca or cursing stones, which were used to bring down malediction on one's enemies. Some lines from Samuel Ferguson's poem on the Burial of King Cormac indicate that this was a custom going back to ancient times. Ferguson put into verse a story of pre-Christian Ireland recorded in one of our earliest manuscripts.

> They loosed their curse against the king,
> They cursed him in his flesh and bones,
> And daily in their mystic ring,
> They turned the Maledictive Stones.

The island monastery was founded by Saint

Molaise in the sixth century and while the island was inhabited an ancient image of the saint was held in veneration by the islanders. This is a figure of carved oak, somewhat over four feet in height, worn with age and scarred by the passage of time. It is now in the National Museum in Dublin.

> The young birds and the old birds
> Came flying, heavy and sad;
> Keening in from Tireragh,
> Keening from Ballinafad;
> Keening from Inishmurray,
> Nor stayed for bite or sup;
> This way were all reproved
> Who dig old customs up.

In 'The Ballad of Father O'Hart', Yeats's fascination with place names is evident.

The land at Mullaghmore and Cliffoney was owned by Lord Palmerstown, Prime Minister of England, in the reign of Queen Victoria. He built Classiebawn Castle, which, viewed from a distance, looks like an illustration in a fairy tale. The building of the castle was completed by his stepson, William Francis Cooper, Lord Mount Temple. It passed from him to his nephew, the Honourable Evelyn Ashley, and from his heir to his granddaughter Edwina, wife of Earl Mountbatten of Burma. She died in 1960. It is still the holiday home of the Mountbatten family.

Creevykeel—not far from Cliffoney—is the site of the finest example of a full court-cairn in Ireland. It was excavated in 1935 by the Fourth Harvard Archaeological Expedition. Among the primary grave-goods were plain, shouldered neolithic pottery, decorated, shouldered ware, leaf-shaped arrow-heads, hollow scrapers, and polished stone axe-heads.

This district is full of interest for the archaeologist; there are a variety of court-cairns, an earth ring and a stone fort in the area. There is an early cross-slab at Saint Bridgid's Well and a tradition that she lived there for some time. From Hannon's Cross, near Cliffoney, a road leads straight to Gleniff and the Cliffs of Annacoona, the north face of Ben Bulben, famous among botanists for its rare plants of the alpine species. The horse-shoe drive into the Gleniff Valley brings one under the strange shape of Ben Weskin, and to the foot of Truskmore, the highest peak in the range. High up on the side of the mountain facing north, there is a natural cavern in the limestone rock, which is called the 'bed of Diarmuid and Grainne'.

The River Drowes runs into the sea near Bundoran, about seven miles north of Cliffoney. It was in a monastery at Bundrowes (the foot of the Drowes) that the Four Masters laboured at the Annals. Ballyshannon is three miles further north in County Donegal (Tir Conaill) the territory of the O'Donnells. This was the home of William Allingham, the poet who inspired Yeats as a young man to study the country beliefs and pre-historic traditions of Sligo, and to express the modest wish of doing for Sligo what William Allingham had done for Ballyshannon. At a much later date Yeats compared Allingham and Thomas Davis, and their two different kinds of love of Ireland. He said:

In Allingham I find the entire emotion of the place one grew up in which I felt as a child.

Davis on the other hand was concerned with ideas of Ireland, with conscious patriotism.

He sums up in favour of the former, saying:

> This love was instinctive and left the soul free. If I could have kept it and yet never felt the influence of Young Ireland I had given a more profound picture of Ireland in my work.

Returning home to Sligo the traveller will pass by Drumcliff. Of all the places mentioned, this is the one most closely associated with Yeats. For here, in the graveyard beside the church where his great-grandfather had been rector, the poet lies at rest. He died in the South of France in January 1939 at the age of seventy-three and was buried at Roquebrune. The Second World War prevented his body being moved to Ireland for reinterment until 1948. He now lies in Drumcliff churchyard, in accordance with his wishes, under a stone which bears the last lines of the epitaph he himself wrote:

> Under bare Ben Bulben's head
> In Drumcliff churchyard Yeats is laid.
> An ancestor was rector there
> Long years ago, a church stands near,
> By the road an ancient cross.
> No marble, no conventional phrase;
> On limestone quarried near the spot
> By his command these words are cut:
>> Cast a cold eye
>> On life, on death.
>> Horseman, pass by!

The village straggles attractively along the Bundoran road, under the lower slopes of Ben Bulben. The fine High Cross and the Round Tower, of

which only the lower portion remains, recall the
monastery founded here in 574 by Saint Columcille. The High Cross is thought to be of the tenth
century; the annals of this monastery are recorded
by the Four Masters up to the year 1503. It was
known as Drumcliff of the Crosses and to it was
attached a house of studies, frequented even by
foreigners, who came from afar to imbibe
knowledge at this celebrated school. A broken
cross, which was originally at Drumcliff, is in the
National Museum, Dublin. It has figure carvings
treated in a similar way to those on the Iona-
Kildalton crosses. This is an interesting link with
the tradition that has claimed a close connection
between Drumcliff and the famous Columban
foundation of the inner Hebrides. There is also
the shaft of a tall, plain, stone cross, erected on
the corner-stone of the graveyard at Drumcliff.
Saint Columcille's attachment to Drumcliff is expressed in a few lines of a poem attributed to him
and translated into English:

> Beloved to my heart, also is the west,
> Drumcliff at Culcinne's Strand.

Drumcliff is the centre of an area which meant
a great deal to Yeats, for he saw there both tradi-

tional social values and a living mythological inheritance.

Frank O'Connor wrote on the occasion of the poet's re-burial:

> Today we can think of his return only as a completion of a work long-planned, the crowning of a life which was like a great work of art, nobly conceived, nobly executed and now brought to a triumphant conclusion . . . For it was part of the work of art as he saw it that he who took inspiration from the landscape and people of Sligo should return to them in the end.

VIII

COUNTY ROSCOMMON

When Yeats visited Douglas Hyde at his home in Frenchpark, County Roscommon, the two young men had much in common. During his visit to Ratra House, Yeats learned much of the ancient lore and legends of this part of Connacht from Hyde, who later was to become the first President of Ireland. He visited Rathcroghan, the site of the ancient palace of the kings of Connacht. It was, in pre-Christian and early Christian times, a royal capital; many of the kings who reigned at Tara were crowned there. It was the royal stronghold of Queen Maeve, whose wars against the Ulster men are celebrated in *The Tain*, one of the great epic poems. Yeats wrote many times of Cruachan or Rathcroghan:

> Maeve the great Queen was pacing to and fro
> Between the walls covered with beaten bronze
> In the high house at Cruachan.

Lough Key near Boyle is a lake of many romantic legends. Yeats went fishing on Lough Key with Douglas Hyde. He saw the uninhabited castle of the MacDermots on The Rock, and dreamed of establishing there a 'Castle of the Heroes'. He saw the uninhabited castle as the meeting-place of a new cult which would relate the tents of Theosophy and the Golden Dawn to the Ireland of his day. It was part of his dream, which was never fulfilled, that the finest minds in Ireland would visit the castle and absorb the teachings of the mystical order which was to have its headquarters there. His notion was to link the basic truths of Christianity to those of a more ancient faith, and to establish the 'Castle of the Heroes' as a place

where twentieth-century Ireland might commune
with its mystical past. He tried to interest Maud
Gonne in the idea of this shrine of Irish traditions,
where only those who had proved their devotion
to Ireland could gain admission. Joseph Hone
relates a charming account of their last meeting,
in old age, when the poet could only rise from
the armchair with difficulty to greet her:

> As she got up to leave he referred to the
> glorious ends they had once sought together.
> "Maud", he said, "we should have gone on
> with our 'Castle of the Heroes'." She was so
> surprised at his remembering that she could
> not reply. She had thought him contaminated
> with the British Empire.

On Insula Trinitas or Trinity Island are the
ruins of the Abbey of the Trinity founded by the
White Canons, where the Annals of Lough Ce
were compiled. Here, too, are the two ash-trees
that entwined their branches over the graves of
Una MacDermot, daughter of the last chieftain of
the Rock, and MacCostello of Moygara, the ill-
starred lovers about whom there are a variety of
legends and whose story inspired the lovely Gaelic
lament 'Una Bhan'. Yeats has woven the story of
their love into his tale in *The Secret Rose*, which
he called 'Proud Costello, MacDermot's Daughter,
and the Bitter Tongue'.

The beautiful demesne of Rockingham is on the
southern shore of the lake. Rockingham House was
accidentally burned down in 1957. The older house
designed by John Nash was burned down in 1863.
Boyle Abbey, the ruined thirteenth-century Cistercian Monastery, gives beauty and character to the
little town. The Abbey was a place of importance

and influence in medieval Connacht. Donnach Mor O'Dalaigh, the celebrated bardic poet, is among the illustrious dead buried within its walls.

The church was consecrated in 1218, and is Romanesque, with some Gothic features. There are also the remains of the gate-house, porter's lodge, cloisters, kitchen and cellars beneath the refectory and sacristy. Cromwellian troopers occupied the Abbey in 1659, and the names carved on the doorways of the porter's lodge are said to be theirs.

Lough Arrow is separated from Lough Key by the Curlew Hills. On the eastern shore is the ruined Dominican Abbey of Ballindoon, built in 1507. Within its walls, there is an interesting monument, dedicated to the memory of Terence MacDonough, 'The Great Counsellor', dated 1737. Ballindoon (the town of the Doon) gets its name from the great cairn of Heapstown, which is not far from the prehistoric battlefield of Moytirra or Moytura, where according to the old books, the Tuatha de Danann finally defeated the Firbolgs. Lying to the north of Kilmactranny, the battlefield is a bleak tableland about one mile square strewn with heaps of stone. There is a fine portal dolmen at Carrickglass, and the remarkable passage grave cemetery of Carrowkeel is across country on the Bricklieve Mountain.

Hollybrook House on the shore of Lough Arrow was the scene of the romantic adventure of Willie Reilly and his 'Colleen Bawn', (the daughter of Colonel ffolliot), celebrated by the nineteenth-century novelist, William Carleton. The history of this area is covered in detail in *The Castle of Heroes* by James P. McGarry, LL.B., published by *The Roscommon Herald.*

Castlerea in County Roscommon was the birth-place of Sir William Wilde, father of Oscar Wilde. It is also the seat of the O'Conor Don family, who have their home at Clonalis House. The present holder of the title is the Reverend Charles O'Conor, S.J. This is one of the old Gaelic families tracing their lineage back to Turlough Mor O'Conor, King of Ireland. His son, Roderick O'Conor, who died in 1198, was the last High King of Ireland. The O'Conors joined with the MacDermotroes of Alderford in being the chief patrons of Turlough O'Carolan, and have among their forebears Charles O'Conor, 1710-1790, an authority on the language, history and antiquities of Ireland.

IX

COUNTIES GALWAY AND MAYO

When Yeats was about thirty years old, he brought
Arthur Symons, the editor of *The Savoy*, on a
sight-seeing tour of Sligo. From Sligo they travelled
to County Galway to visit Coole House, Tulira
Castle and Roxborough House, three great demesnes which lay within easy reach of each other.

Roxborough, the home of Lady Gregory's
family, the Persses, was burnt down during the
Civil War.

Tulira Castle is now the home of Lord Hemp-
hill, a collateral descendant of the writer Edward
Martyn, whose influence as a patron of the arts
lingers on in this part of the country. It may be
seen in the Cathedral of Saint Brendan at Lough-
rea, and in the Martyn Memorial Window which

was his gift to the little Catholic church of Laban.

Of Coole House itself, Yeats prophetically wrote:

> Here, traveller, scholar, poet, take your stand
> When all those rooms and passages are gone,
> When nettles wave upon a shapeless mound
> And saplings root among the broken stone.

This house was the hospitable home of Lady Gregory and her son, Robert, poet, artist, and airman. Her nephew, Hugh Lane, the distinguished art-dealer, was a welcome guest, as were her friends, W. B. Yeats, Jack Yeats, John Millington Synge, Douglas Hyde, Edward Martyn from Tulira, and George Moore from Carra Lake near Ballinrobe.

The house is now the ruin Yeats foresaw. Despite pleas which were made for its preservation, it was pulled down in 1941, and now only a few broken walls remain. There is, however, one interesting relic of the great days of Coole, the copper beech in the grounds on which many of Lady Gregory's famous guests carved their initials. It is still possible to identify those of George Bernard Shaw, Sean O'Casey, William Butler Yeats, Jack Butler Yeats, A.E. (George Russell), Katharine Tynan Hinkson, Violet Martin ('Sommerville and Ross'), Robert Gregory and Augusta Gregory.

Coole was of great importance to Yeats. A fairly conventional eighteenth-century mansion set among lakes, woods and formal gardens, he first made a long visit there in 1897, a year which found him emotionally and physically exhausted. Lady Gregory nursed him back to health and for the next twenty years Coole was to be practically his home. The association between the poet and Lady Gregory led that indomitable woman to participate actively in the Irish Literary Movement, and to commence writing her plays. Many of the poems in *The Wild Swans at Coole, The Green Helmet* and *Responsibilities* belong to this period. Thoor Ballylee (Ballylee Castle), five miles northeast of Gort, in the barony of Kiltartan, is a sixteenth-century tower built in the Norman style, which Yeats bought for thirty-five pounds.

> An ancient bridge, and a more ancient tower,
> A farmhouse that is sheltered by its wall . . .
> A winding stair, a chamber arched with stone,
> A grey stone fireplace with an open hearth,
> A candle and written page.

The tower became for the poet, not only a solitary retreat, but also a physical symbol of mental solitude and questing. He saw Thoor Ballylee as a place of austere discipline from which he might in his old age influence younger generations.

The four-storey stone tower has a castellated roof and stands by a stream. Yeats had the tower and its adjacent cottage and gardens reconstructed. He spent part of each summer there with his family, and from it he could see the woods of Coole. Pacing on its battlements, he saw below the tiny village of Ballylee associated with the beautiful Mary Hynes, celebrated in blind Raftery's Gaelic poem, and put into English by Lady Gregory.

Many of Yeats's great poems came from this time and place: *The Tower*, published in 1928 and *The Winding Stair and Other Poems* (1933).

The tower, for many years dilapidated and neglected, was once again restored in 1965, to commemorate the centenary of the poet's birth. On its walls are inscribed the words Yeats wrote to mark his restoration of the tower:

> I, the poet William Yeats,
> With old mill-boards and sea-green slates,
> And smithy work from the Gort forge,
> Restored this tower for my wife George;
> And may these characters remain
> When all is ruin once again.

A paper by Mary Hanley, on Thoor Ballylee, was published by the Dolmen Press in 1965.

On the sea-coast a few miles from Coole is Durras House, where Yeats and Lady Gregory visited their friend Count Florimond de Basterot to discuss the project of an Irish Theatre. Now Durras House is a Youth Hostel, with a plaque erected in 1961 to commemorate Yeats, Lady Gregory, Edward Martyn and de Basterot.

Further south near Ballyvaughan is the ruined Cistercian Monastery of Corcomroe, founded by Donal O'Brien, King of Limerick in 1180. It contains a number of interesting features including the sculptured tomb said to be that of King Conor O'Brien and above it the effigy of an Abbot. Yeats wrote:

> Close to the altar
> Broken by wind and frost and worn by time
> Donough O'Brien has a tomb, a name in Latin.

It is near Corcomroe that the young man meets the ghostly lovers, Diarmuid and Dervorgilla in *The Dreaming of the Bones*. Yeats responded to the mystery of the strange rugged landscape of the Burren, and to the 'cold Clare rock, and Galway rock and thorn'. Neither tree, nor bush, nor grass, grows on these gaunt, grey, limestone hills, yet in the spring and early summer the Burren is carpeted with a profusion of wild flowers.

In later years Oliver St. John Gogarty's house at Renvyle out on the Connemara coast became a meeting-place for artists and writers. Yeats and the painter Augustus John were among those who visited this beautifully situated house. Like Yeats, Gogarty was a member of the first Irish Senate, and was a supremely gifted man; a distinguished visitor from Italy said he recalled for him the great Italians of the Quattrocento. There is no doubt about Yeats's friendship and admiration; it is recorded in the poet's Introduction to *The Oxford Book of Modern Verse*, a book which caused such a flurry in its day. Now Renvyle is a hotel, and Gogarty lies buried in the churchyard nearby.

John Millington Synge drew much of his inspiration from the Aran Islands off the Galway coast. He met Yeats for the first time a few days before Christmas, 1896, in a student hostel in the Latin quarter of Paris. Yeats advised him to go to Aran, which he had just visited himself, and to live there among the people. He told the unknown Irishman: 'Express a life that has never found expression'. About this time also, Synge met Maud Gonne, and she and Yeats turned his interest back from European to Irish writers. His first visit to Aran was in 1898, although an uncle of his had been a Protestant missionary there. This visit changed an unknown writer into a playwright of international fame. He heard there the stories which gave him the raw material for *In the Shadow of the Glen* and *The Playboy of the*

77

Western World. The first he was to transfer to Wicklow and the second to Mayo. From the people of Aran he learned the rich English which is distinctively his, an English which owes much to its Gaelic substratum. Patrick MacDonagh's cottage on Inishmaan, one of the islands, is still very much as it was when Synge stayed there.

This brief description of the area surrounding Sligo indicates how many writers were within fairly easy reach of Yeats. Douglas Hyde, Lady Gregory, Edward Martyn, George Moore, Oliver Gogarty, John Millington Synge; these were among the living, but there were memories also of Wilde and Goldsmith, and of the legion of known or forgotten Gaelic poets and annalists. Between all these and William Butler Yeats there was a cross-pollination of genius which gave that part of Ireland in those years a distinguished and permanent place in literary history.

APPENDIX I

MEANINGS OF PLACENAMES

Alt or Alt dubh: Black Glen (under Knocknarea)
Beltra Strand: Strand mouth, also named Traig Eothaile
— strand of Eothaile
Ballysadare: Baile easa dara—The town of the waterfall
Ballinafad: Bel an atha fada — The mouth of the long
ford
Ballygawley: Baile ui Dalaigh — O'Daly's town
Ben Bulben: The peak of Conal Gulban
Carrowmore: The great quarter
Castle Dargan: Caiseal deargain — Deargan's stone fort
Collooney: Cuil Maoile — nook of the Maoile
Cleveragh: Cliabrach — the place of the basket makers
Culleenamore: Coillin na mbodar — the little wood of
the deafening noise
Cummeen: Commons
Croagh: A 'Rick' — rick-like hill on a mountain
Croghan: Cruachan — diminutive of Croagh
Dooney Dock: The rock like a little fort
Dromahaire: Druim Dha Eithiar — The ridge of the two
air-demons
Glencar: The glen of the two pillar stones
Heart Lake: Loc na croidhe
Innisfree: Inis fraoic — island of heather
Innishmurray: Island of Murragagh
Kilmacowen: The church of the sons of Eoin
Kilvarnet: The church in the gap
Knocknarea: The flat-topped hill
    (*meaning disputed*): The hill of the king
                          The hill of the moon
                          The hill of executions
                          The hill of storms
Knocknashee: Cnoch na Siadh — The hill of the faery
Lissadell: Lios a' doill — Fort of the blind man
Lugnagall: Lug na ngall — hollow of the foreigners
Magheraboy: Machaire buidhe — The yellow plain
Manorhamilton: Old name Cluainin Ui Ruairc —
    O'Rourke's Little Field
Miscaun Meadhbh: Maeve's Cairn
Rosses: Peninsulas
Sleuth or Slish Wood: Slios or sliu — the wood on the
slope or slant

Sliabh da ein: The mountain of the two birds
Sligo: Shelly, shelly river
Tireragh: Fiachres district
Ocris Head: The point of the horses
Enniscrone: Watershed Island
Sruth in aghaidh an aird: The stream against the height
Tobernalt: The cliff well
Tubbercurry: The well of the whirlpool
Ox Mountains: Sliamh-dhamh, corruption of sliabh-
    ghamh — stormy mountains
Tullaghan: Little hill

APPENDIX II
THE PLACENAMES RELATED TO YEATS'S POEMS AND PLAYS

*Titles of works by W. B. Yeats in this appendix
are printed in italics*

POEMS

Alt, The glen at: *The Man and the Echo*

Beltra Strand: *The Valley of the Black Pig*

Ballysadare: *The Ballad of Father O'Hart*

Ballinafad: *The Ballad of Father O'Hart*

Ballygawley: *Red Hanrahan's Curse* (in *Mythologies*)

Ben Bulben: *On a Political Prisoner; Towards Break of Day; Alternative Song for the Severed Head; Under Ben Bulben; The Mountain Tomb; The Tower*

Carrowmore: *The Wanderings of Oisin: 'the Firbolgs' burial-mounds'*

Castle Dargan: *The King of the Great Clock Tower; Red Hanrahan's Curse* (in *Mythologies*)

Collooney: *The Ballad of Father O'Hart*

Coole: *In the Seven Woods; To a Friend whose Work has come to Nothing; The Wild Swans at Coole; In Memory of Major Robert Gregory; An Irish Airman Foresees his Death; Shepherd and Goatherd; To a Squirrel at Kyle-Na-No; Coole Park 1929; Coole Park and Ballylee, 1931; For Anne Gregory; The Shadowy Waters* (Introductory Lines)

Cleveragh: *Down by the Salley Gardens*

Culleenamore: *Cuchulain's Fight with the Sea*

Cummen Strand: *Red Hanrahan's Song about Ireland*

Croghan (Cruachan): *The Hour before Dawn; The Dancer at Cruachan and Cro-Patrick; Tom at Cruachan; The Old Age of Queen Maeve*

Cro Patrick (Co. Mayo): *The Dancer at Cruachan and Cro-Patrick*

Drumahaire (Co. Leitrim): *The Man who Dreamed of Faeryland*

Drumcliff: *Are You Content?; Under Ben Bulben*

Glencar: *The Stolen Child*

Hart Lake: *The Host of the Air*

Innisfree: *The Lake Isle of Innisfree*

Innishmurray: *The Ballad of Father O'Hart*

Kilvarnet: *The Fiddler of Dooney*
Knocknarea: *The Hosting of the Sidhe; Red Hanrahan's Song about Ireland; The Ballad of Father O'Hart; Alternative Song for the Severed Head; The Wanderings of Oisin; The Valley of the Black Pig; The Black Tower*
Knocknashee: *The Ballad of Father O'Hart*
Lissadell: *The Man who Dreamed of Faeryland; In Memory of Eva Gore-Booth and Con Markiewicz; Easter 1916; The Valley of the Black Pig* (notes)
Lugnagall: *The Man who Dreamed of Faeryland*
Magheraboy: *The Fiddler of Dooney*
Rosses: *The Stolen Child; At Algeciras — A Meditation Upon Death; Alternative Song for the Severed Head; Three Songs to the One Burden; The Meditation of the Old Fisherman; The Black Tower*
Raghley Head: *Tom O'Roughley* (only in title)
Scanavin: *The Man who Dreamed of Faeryland*
Sleuth Wood or Slish Wood: *The Stolen Child*
Sliabh-Da-Ein: *The Hosting of the Sidhe* (notes)
Sligo: *Under Saturn; Are You Content?; In Memory of Alfred Pollexfen; The Fiddler of Dooney; The Meditation of the Old Fisherman*
Thoor Ballylee: *A Prayer on going into my House; A Prayer for my Daughter; To be Carved on a Stone at Thoor Ballylee; The Tower; Meditations in Time of Civil War; Blood and the Moon; A Dialogue of Self and Soul*
Tireragh: *The Ballad of Father O'Hart*

PLAYS

Ballygawley
Collooney
Kilmacowen
Ocris Head: *The Land of Heart's Desire*

Enniscrone
Ballina
Killala: *Cathleen Ni Houlihan*

Tubber
Tubbercurry: *The Pot of Broth*

The Ox Mountains
Tullaghan Well
The Hawk's Rock
Beltra Strand: *At the Hawk's Well*

Dromahaire (indirect reference to the story of Diarmuid
and Dervorgilla): *The Dreaming of the Bones*

Castle Dargan (possibly): *Pugatory*

Kinvara
Gort: *The King's Threshold; Deirdre* (In Memory of
Robert Gregory)

Finvara
Corcomroe: *The Dreaming of the Bones; The Words
Upon the Window-Pane* (In Memory of Lady
Gregory)

MYTHOLOGIES

Kiltartan
Ballylee
Kinvara: *Dust hath closed Helen's Eye; Stories of Red
Hanrahan* (Rewritten in 1907 with Lady Gregory's
help)

APPENDIX III

BIBLIOGRAPHY

Yeats, William Butler: *Collected Poems; Collected Plays; Mythologies; Autobiographies; John Sherman and Dhoya; Irish Fairy and Folk Tales*

Yeats, W. B. *chosen by*: *The Oxford Book of Modern Verse*

Yeats, Jack Butler: *Sligo*

Allingham, Hugh (*Ed*): *Captain Cuellar's Adventures in Connacht and Ulster A.D. 1588*

Allt & Alspach: *The Variorum Edition of the Poems of W. B. Yeats*

Bjersby, Birgit: *The Cuchulainn legend in the works of W. B. Yeats*

Corkery, Daniel: *The Hidden Ireland*

Dillon, Myles (*Ed*): *Early Irish Sagas; Early Irish Society*

Hanley, Mary: *Thoor Ballylee*

Henn, Thomas Rice: *The Lonely Tower*

Henry, Francoise: *Irish High Crosses*

Hone, Joseph: *W. B. Yeats 1865 - 1939*

Joyce, P. W.: *Irish Names of Places*

Kilgannon, Tadhg: *Sligo and its Surroundings*

Killanin & Duignan: *Shell Guide to Ireland*

Knott, Eleanor: *Irish Classical Poetry; The Bardic Poems of Tadhg Dall O'Huiginn*

Lectures, Thomas Davis: *Great Books of Ireland*

McGarry, James P.: *The Castle of Heroes*

McTernan, John C.: *Historic Sligo*

Marreco, Ann: *The Rebel Countess*

Miller, Liam (*Ed*): *The Dolmen Press Yeats Centenary Papers*

Moody & Martin (*Ed*): *The Course of Irish History*

Murphy, William M.: *The Yeats Family and the Pollexfens of Sligo*

O'Connor, Frank: *The Little Monasteries; Kings, Lords and Commons*

O'Connor, Ulick: *Oliver St. John Gogarty*

O'Cuiv, Brian: *Seven Centuries of Irish Learning*

O'Rorke, Terence: *History of Sligo, town and county; History of Ballisodare & Kilvarnet*

O'Sullivan, Donal: *Carolan, The Life, Times and Music of an Irish Harper*
Robinson, Lennox: *Bryan Cooper*
Stallworthy, Jon: *Yeats's Last Poems*
Van Voris, Jacqueline: *Constance Markiewicz*
Wakeman, W. F.: *Innismurray*
Wood-Martin, W. G.: *History of Sligo — County and Town*

APPENDIX IV
PLACE AND PLACENAMES IN THE POETRY OF W. B. YEATS*

Yeats's sense of place and his poetical use of placenames are a source of endless fascination for those of us who live in that part of Ireland now called the 'Yeats Country'. Many of the placenames are beautiful in themselves but in the setting of a Yeats poem they sparkle and glow with an added beauty, evoking in some magical way the very atmosphere of the place. Lissadell, Glencar, Knocknarea, Ballisadare are all there — each with its own special quality.

> He slept under the hill of Lugnagall;
> And might have known at last unhaunted sleep
> Under that cold and vapour-turbaned steep.

It is difficult to imagine a more evocative line to convey the atmosphere of that gaunt hill overlooking the Glencar valley. The decorative beauty of Yeats's early poetry owed much to his preoccupation with the wonders of nature and to his discovery of the hidden riches in the traditions and lore of the country folk. He expressed this in *Ideas of Good and Evil,*

> One's verses should hold, as in a mirror, the colours of one's own climate and scenery . . . (and) make every lake or mountain a man can see from his own door an excitement in his imagination.

As his art became less decorative, it became more eloquent, more authoritative; and he entered

*Reprinted from the Annual Report and Bulletin (No. 5, 1970) of the Yeats Society of Japan. Tokyo 1970. pp. 9–11.

into the period of his great achievement. Once
again a sense of place is a characteristic of the
great poems of his middle years. It is no longer
the Sligo of his youth but the countryside south
of Galway — Thoor Ballylee and Coole Park —
from here he forged the great symbols which are
of universal significance. One English critic, writing of this Lady Gregory country, said 'it is not
ridiculous to go on pilgrimage there, if only to see
how closely Yeats's descriptions correspond to
the facts.'

The importance of place and placenames was
also a feature of the literature of ancient Ireland.
It may be that Yeats learned this from the Gaelic
poets, for it must be remembered that at about the
age of twenty he deliberately set out to make
himself an Irish poet. This may come as a surprise
to some, who are unaware that at that time the
old Gaelic tradition was almost forgotten and
most Irishmen were educated in the great tradition
of English literature. Yeats gave expression to this
sentiment when he wrote 'To Ireland in the
Coming Times'.

As the end of his life drew near, his thoughts
seemed to return to the places he knew in youth,
and in these last weeks he wrote 'The Black
Tower' and 'Under Ben Bulben'.

When Professor Shotaro Oshima visited William
Butler Yeats at his home in Dublin, in the summer
of 1938, the poet advised his guest from Japan to
visit if possible Sligo, Mayo, Galway and Clare
and so on. Five months later, Shotaro Oshima
stood on the deck of the Aquitania in mid-
Atlantic; he had just heard of the poet's death
and he has recorded his impressions of that
moment,

> I gazed on the rolling waves and at the most glorious sunset that I had seen in years. The sight imparted a feeling which seemed as if I had received a sad and solemn blow deep in my heart.
>
> (*W. B. Yeats and Japan* by Shotaro Oshima.)

For many there was no sun on that day. Remember Auden's

> He disappeared in the dead of winter;
> The brooks were frozen, the airports almost deserted,
> The snow disfigured the public statues;
> The mercury sank in the mouth of the dying day.
> What instruments we have agree
> The day of his death was a dark cold day.

To these two impressions I add my own. In my journal, under the date of 28 January 1939, I noted that I spent the day at Rosses Point, County Sligo, where I saw the sun set in a glorious blaze of crimson, as it sank slowly into a deep blue mirror-like sea unruffled by the slightest wind. The golfers were out on the links usually deserted in January. Under Ben Bulben the day of Yeats's death was not a dark, cold, day; it was a remarkable day for the time of year, mild, bright, and beautiful.

And W. H. Auden wrote:

> Now Ireland has her madness and her weather still,
> For poetry makes nothing happen.